MW01278293

Published at Pacific Grove, California

Copyright © 2016 by Candid Camera, Inc.
All rights reserved.

No part of this book may be reproduced, stored in a retrieval system,
or transmitted in any form, by any means, including mechanical,
electronic, photocopying, recording, or otherwise, without prior written
permission of the copyright holder.

Printed in the United States of America.

Candid Camera
        8 Decades of Smiles / by Candid Camera

        ISBN-13: 978-0692796160 (Candid Camera)

        ISBN-10: 0692796169

8 Decades of Smiles

On a rare day off, Allen Funt took his family to the beach. As he gazed at the ocean, a woman adjusted her swim suit and it briefly slipped down in front. Catching Allen's glance, she rushed over and slapped him in the face. "Don't you dare show that on TV!" she exclaimed.

It was a startling and yet telling moment: Allen's face and TV show were high in the public's consciousness.

Candid Camera crosses the generations as no other show in television history. It is the only entertainment series to have produced new episodes in each of the last eight decades—from Allen's TV debut in 1948, to Peter Funt's series on TV Land in 2014. The library contains episodes produced for CBS,

NBC and ABC. On cable the list includes HBO, TV Land, PAX and Playboy. There have also been Candid radio shows, feature films, DVD collections, plus books and record albums.

Allen was joined by his son, Peter, as co-host in the mid-1980s. They appeared together until 1993.

Viewers often assume that the word *candid* means tricky; in fact, it means *honest*. And that was Allen's focus: to present an honest view of how people react to a wide variety of situations. It's not scientific, but it often comes close. The show's mission statement is captured in the writing of the poet Robert Burns who observed that the greatest gift is to "see ourselves as others see us."

About that cover photo...

For a show that prides itself on candor, the photo of Allen and Peter on our cover is about as dishonest as anything could be. Designers wanted a shot of the two Funts side-by-side and they elected to use a photo of Allen from the 1980s and one of Peter from the early 2000s. They pasted the heads on bodies of two male models seated in director's chairs. (The photo at the top of this page is legit.)

If you look closely at the fake, the hands are the biggest tip that something's not right. Also, Peter's headshot is flipped—giving a mirror image of his actual appearance.

"I brought the photo home to show my wife, Amy," Peter recalls. "You'd think my own wife would recognize the fact that it's someone else's body. But what did Amy say? 'Where did you get that tie?'"

1940s

audio editors as they sift through hours of audio recordings, which were edited painstakingly.

Among the early Candid Microphone gags, an electrician arrives at a wealthy businessman's office and is asked to make an "electric chair." Another scene, a moving company is called to pick up a trunk that is emitting strange moaning sounds. And another, a locksmith must remove a lock that a man uses to chain his secretary to her desk. In all three cases it was generally proved that when a business opportunity presents itself and money is involved, it's wise to avoid asking too many questions.

In his book, "Candidly, Allen Funt," published in 1994, Allen reflected on the uncharted territory. "In those days," he wrote, "the public was fascinated by the idea of recording equipment that was so small it could be hidden [although compared to today's miniature devices the gear back then was big and bulky]. Remember this was the beginning of the Cold War and fears of Russians spying on the U.S. were constantly on people's minds. Publicity for Candid Microphone always mentioned how the microphone was hidden. I would occasionally get contacted by agents from foreign countries who wanted tips on improving their surveillance operations."

Allen originally believed it would be enough to eavesdrop on the conversations of ordinary people. But in early tries, the dialogue proved too dull. One day, while Allen was hanging a mike from the drill apparatus in a dentist's office, a patient entered and mistook him for the dentist. As the woman began to complain about her wisdom teeth, Allen slid into the role and chided her gently. It wasn't very funny but it confirmed that a provocateur was needed in the scenes.

The New York Herald Tribune wrote that Candid Microphone was, "a wonderful sport, like looking through keyholes but capable of infinitely greater variety." The critic went on to say, "Wait till they get the Candid Television Camera. You won't be safe in your own bathtub."

Candid Microphone begins
June 28, 1947

The American Broadcasting Company presents...
THE CANDID MICROPHONE!
(Theme music in and under)
Put a man on a stage and he tries to imitate life. Let a woman know she's broadcasting and she's anything but herself. But go off the stage into the world, hide the microphone and it will capture candid glimpses of people never before heard on the air. That's exactly what this program aims to bring you. We do not intend to spy or pry into people's private lives. We seek nothing but reality and we capture just that.

So began the first Candid Microphone broadcast, at 7:30 p.m. on a Saturday night in June 1947. Although it was a simple radio program, the process in those days was complex, as evident in the photo above. Allen supervises

The radio show was a modest hit, and continued for several years, even after Allen began the TV version in 1948.

"Candid Camera quickly showed me the enormous power of televised images," Allen recalled. "Now, of course, audiences were able to see people's faces instead of just hearing their voices. It was the faces of ordinary people—confronted by unusual events—that would captivate viewers for years. These faces were filled with surprise, with bewilderment, with thought and, at times, with anger."

It was never the show's intention to make people angry, although the earliest episodes in the 1940s sought to provoke somewhat heated conversation. "My role," said Allen, "gradually turned into that of a heckler who would tease, cajole, and shock unsuspecting people...We kept trying to vary the mood of our candid studies, but by the end of our first year of broadcasting, our most-remembered episodes were those in which people came within an inch of hitting me in the nose."

Gradually, the focus shifted to good-natured fun and social observation. An iconic sequence that perfectly captured both was *The Talking Mailbox.* Shot on a street corner in New York City, people mailing letters were surprised to hear the mailbox "talking" to them. Nowadays, everything talks to us—from our computers to our cars—

CANDID TRIVIA: when the show began in 1948, it was the very first program on the fledgling ABC Network.

but in the forties, the idea of a mailbox that could speak was unimaginable. The highlight of the sequence came when a man spoke to the mailbox and then stopped a passing cop and excitedly told him the box was talking. But the mailbox fell silent. "Speak up! Speak up!" the fellow implored but there was not a word as the cop shook his head and walked away.

Reviews for the television series were largely favorable. *Variety* said: "Candid Camera is even better than it was as a (radio) attraction." *Time* wrote: "Funt is a highly resourceful ad-libber, and his victims are life itself, about as pure as the screen can ever catch it."

The critic was spot-on in singling out Allen's ability to improvise—which is especially difficult when you're trying to add to the humor without upstaging the unsuspecting star.

Once Allen played the clerk at a lost-and-found department. A man called to ask about shoes he had left on a commuter train. He was told they had been found, but when he reached the counter Allen informed him they were lost again. With pure sarcasm the fellow said, "Well, if you happen to trip over them, please let me know."

Allen replied, "Sir, that's one thing about our department. Once we lose something, it stays lost."

CANDID MICROPHONE

MOVIES' MOST INTRIGUING SHORT!

SERIES 4, No. 6

ANOTHER LAUGH-FILLED ENTERTAINMENT THRILL!

"Candid Mike's" on the prowl again... as he pries into the private lives of unsuspecting every-day people to catch them hilariously off-guard!

◀ "THEY CAN'T DO THIS TO ME!"

A GLAMOR GIRL— MISS AMERICA 1970!

A REAL SPORTS-STORE SPORT! ◀

FILMED WITH CONCEALED CAMERAS!
Based on Allen E. Funt's radio program, "CANDID MICROPHONE"

A COLUMBIA SHORT-SUBJECT PRESENTATION

"As fascinating as any other form of eavesdropping" ~ TIME MAGAZINE

"Funt's batting average for laughs is well above average" ~ READER'S DIGEST

"A unique program" ~ NEWSWEEK MAGAZINE

"Freshest program devised in years" ~ N.Y. WORLD-TELEGRAM

Candid Movie Shorts
1948

At about the time Candid Microphone came to television, Allen also began creating Candid "short subjects"—15-minute films that theaters typically ran before the feature. Rather than calling the shorts *Candid Camera,* Columbia Pictures decided to use the name *Candid Microphone*, since at that time the radio show was far better known than the TV series.

The un-subtle poster shown at the left was displayed in movie theater lobbies. It calls the program "Movies' most intriguing short!" And, "Another laugh-filled entertainment thrill." It rightly states that the shorts were based on the radio program, but it credits "Allen E. Funt." In fact, Allen's middle initial is "A," for Albert.

The movie shorts played in theaters periodically over the next six years. Most of the filmed vignettes were the same as were being used on the television show, but since TV audiences were so tiny at that time there was little chance of anyone fretting over seeing the same material in two places.

Meanwhile, Candid Camera bounced from ABC to NBC and then to CBS—all during a fairly short period at the end of the forties.

During these early years, the show experimented with different ways to censor occasional bad language. On radio, Allen's wife Evelyn had recorded the word "Censored," which was spliced into the program. Audiences seemed to find that funny, so Allen began using the technique to mask perfectly clean words. The real network censors wouldn't stand for it, insisting that no one is allowed to censor clean language.

Large cans of film containing Candid Microphone sequences are delivered in Manhattan in 1949.

1950s

Candid Camera episodes from the early fifties are in many ways the most mysterious—even to members of the Funt family. They were produced for syndication (distributed to individual stations rather than carried on a network). And, little effort was made to save the footage. Some 25 years later Allen cleaned out his storage vault and discarded much material.

The camera and sound recorders back in the fifties were bulky and difficult to conceal. Even more challenging was disguising the bright lights needed to shoot indoors. One trick Allen hit upon was to light another area of the room—away from the scene being photographed—so brightly that the spot where the filming took place seemed less suspicious by comparison.

Although much of the footage is gone, stories from the period remain, such as the time Allen played a clerk in a pet shop when a man came in seeking to sell his cocker spaniel. The fellow explained that he lived in a third-floor walk-up apartment and was no longer able to take the dog up and down for walks. Trying to do the right thing, Allen agreed to buy the dog for the full asking price.

What followed was a flood of mail, much of it the nastiest in Candid Camera's history. Many people were furious at the man for trying to sell his pet. Others were angry at Allen for buying it. Others were mad at the building for not having an elevator, and a few were upset that the dog required so many walks!

In the summer of 1953, NBC ran 10 episodes of Candid Camera, hosted by a popular comedian of the day named Jerry Lester. By mid-decade Allen wrapped all production and decided to take time off. He had no idea that, in a way, things for Candid Camera were just getting started.

Allen took a brief break from TV in the mid-fifties. He and Evelyn had moved into a house in Croton-on-Hudson, N.Y., about 40 miles north of Manhattan, and they now had three kids: Peter, Patricia and John.

Allen turned his attention to fixing up the property, building a stable for his horses and a basketball court for Peter. His most elaborate project was a model train set so large that it occupied the entire floor of a small building and was so complex that it had several miles of wires. Allen could be found in that room day and night, until one day the layout was complete. At that point Allen lost interest and decided it was time to get back to Candid Camera.

The first production, in 1955, ran as segments on the acclaimed CBS magazine series known as "Omnibus." These clips were less concerned with humor than with studying human nature—which was Allen's primary interest throughout his career.

Next came a batch of appearances on NBC's "Tonight Show," hosted at the time by Jack Paar. In this setting Allen had the opportunity to show footage and then analyze it with the witty and cerebral Paar. The two got along well and a few years later Paar appeared as a guest when Candid Camera returned as a series.

In 1959, Allen's clips became a weekly feature on CBS's "The Garry Moore Show," a variety series that had in its cast Carol Burnett and Durward Kirby, among others. Years later Kirby became Allen's co-host on Candid Camera.

Initially, Allen's concept for Garry Moore's show was to see if celebrities—at first, Moore himself—would be recognized in public. "My theory," Allen explained at the time, "is that a celebrity such as Moore can be placed in a public setting that's out of context with his position and

CANDID TRIVIA: The first "celebrity guest" to appear on Candid Microphone was the horror-film actor Bela Lugosi.

not be noticed." Moore did sequences as a toll collector, a tailor, a store clerk and several other random jobs. No one recognized him, although in 1959 he was among the most popular people on TV. Allen had a tentative deal with CBS to turn that limited concept into a new series but fortunately, that twist on the format didn't happen.

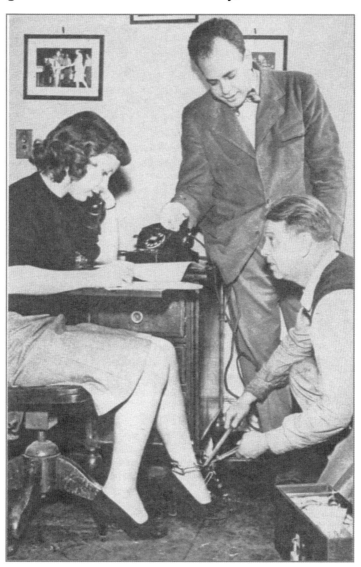

Allen watches as an unsuspecting locksmith removes a chain from a secretary's ankle.

After several weeks, Allen began doing more standard gags, and the results were terrific. The *Chicago Tribune* wrote: "Allen Funt, America's leading sneak, has brought his peekaboo Candid Camera to the Garry Moore variety show, and the result has been a hilarious bit for the program."

Proving that good ideas never get old, the Moore show even tried the "Locksmith" gag. This time Moore played the boss, trying to explain to the locksmith why his secretary was chained to her desk.

At year's end it was announced that CBS was launching Candid Camera as a series, giving Allen his own show again and ushering in a new decades of smiles.

1960s

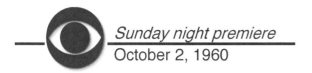

In the new decade, Candid Camera hit its stride as an acclaimed staple in CBS's powerhouse Sunday night lineup. In partnership with Garry Moore's producer, Allen began a seven-year run that yielded some of Candid Camera's highest ratings and brightest moments.

CBS had designed its Sunday schedule for the entire family, beginning with the lovable "Lassie," followed by the eclectic "Ed Sullivan Show," the dramatic series "GE Theater," "The Jack Benny Show," and then, "Candid Camera" followed by the celebrity panel show "What's My Line?"

The first show in 1960 featured the iconic "Car Without a Motor." Singer-actress Dorothy Collins, who became a regular on the show, had the task of steering a car down a hill and into a gas station, where service attendants would discover that there was no engine under the hood.

Two things viewers didn't know: The young teen sitting next to Dorothy operating the audio recorder was Peter Funt; and, although Dorothy did a fine job it was touch-and-go since she didn't have a driver's license! The second show brought more celebrities into the mix, as Jonathan Winters played a complaint manager in a store, and baseball greats Mickey Mantle and Yogi Berra posed as caddies on a golf course.

Selecting a co-host to work alongside Allen proved to be the show's biggest headache. The network picked Arthur Godfrey, the radio star and TV host whom CBS had under contract at the time. Right from the start, Godfrey's personality clashed with Allen's—a situation made worse by the fact that Godfrey had a big ego but a small part in creating the Candid Camera episodes.

"As soon as I heard that Godfrey was chosen,

> **CANDID TRIVIA: Johnny Carson tried out for a role on the show and was told by Allen he'd "never make it in TV."**

I died inside," Allen recalled. I knew that having a co-host with such a big name was asking for trouble...to ask such a powerhouse to play second fiddle to me, on a show where he had nothing to do, was a nasty comedown."

The feud between the two men finally made its way into the papers. Fortunately, Godfrey decided to do some traveling and left the show after its highly successful first season.

His replacement was perfect: a performer Allen had worked with on the Garry Moore show, the affable straight-man Durward Kirby. With Durward the show eased into a smooth style that viewers came to know and love.

To publicize the new show, CBS hired the renowned caricaturist Al Hirschfeld to do a drawing of Allen (opposite page). When Allen saw the drawing he sent the artist a note complaining that, "You made me look like a monkey." Hirschfeld wrote back, "God did that. I only drew it."

Despite his struggles with cartoonists and co-hosts, Allen was riding the wave of popularity. "The advantage of having a hit TV show," said Allen, "is that

Allen and Durward on the set in their New York studio.

the network and sponsors leave you alone." This was during William Paley's time as head of CBS, and the boss was a big fan of the show and Allen's work. Paley's support came in handy at the start of the second season when Allen produced his most controversial and noteworthy episode—an entire broadcast devoted to a visit to the Soviet Union—although initially neither Paley nor anyone at CBS knew of the project.

"I had a rule when dealing with the network," Allen explained. "If I wanted to do something, and I knew the answer would be no, I didn't ask for permission. I just went ahead and did it and dealt with the consequences later."

So it was that in summer 1961 Allen and his small film crew flew to Moscow. They traveled as "tourists," but their objective was to secretly photograph Soviet citizens, about whom most Americans knew little yet feared a great deal. It was a chilling experience, as Allen described it later: "For all we knew, the KGB might throw us in a Siberian prison camp and we'd never be heard from again."

The footage obtained in a week of shooting was enlightening. In one scene, Russians are shown posing for photos at a park in Moscow. Everyone is stern-faced, never smiling. Women, it seemed did the type of hard labor, such as construction, that back home was exclusively done by men. There were few cars; most people in Moscow rode bicycles.

Back in New York, Allen discovered that much of his film had been fogged-over. Apparently the Soviet authorities were wise to his activities. Still, there was enough salvageable footage to make an entire show, which was scheduled for October 15, 1961. When CBS programmers and the show's sponsors saw the program they flatly refused to allow it on the air. They believed that at the height of the Cold War, it would be viewed as unpatriotic to show Soviet citizens in a positive light.

Allen refused to take no for an answer and with only hours remaining until airtime, he screened the show for William Paley. When it was over, Paley said simply, "Let it go. It's important." The show won wide critical acclaim and is preserved on the DVD, "Best of the Sixties, Part 1."

Allen and his crew posed as tourists while secretly photographing the residents of Moscow in ordinary situations. The streets had very few cars; most people walked or rode bikes. The finished half-hour episode was a dramatic departure from Candid Camera's usual fare, but won rave reviews from critics as well as the viewers, who flooded CBS with positive feedback.

As Candid Camera's popularity grew in the sixties, it increasingly became part of pop culture. Even Superman got into the act, when the creators of Action Comics decided to have Clark Kent caught by Allen and his crew!

While the show retained its basic simplicity, some stunts were wonderfully elaborate. There was a car that split in half, a diner stool that sunk into the floor and a building that disappeared. The show also made use of ingenious props such as the umbrella that produced rain, the spoon that melted in coffee, the piano that rolled off stage while it was being played, and the bowling pins that smashed to bits when struck.

Allen built a team of co-pranksters including Tom O'Malley (how much free fruit can Tom eat at a market before the owner makes him buy something?), Bob Schwartz (can he convince motorists that Delaware is "closed for the day"?), Ben Joelson (he's in the park with his own private bench), Dorothy Collins (she asks service station attendants to change the air in her tires), Joey Faye (he's sneezing into a phone and spraying the person on the other end, miles away), Marge Green (in a dress that expanded as she ate), Fannie Flagg (she's a female airline pilot, in the days when there was no such thing).

Allen's son Peter got into the act in the sixties. In one memorable scene he was painted with plaster to be a Roman statue in an art gallery, in another he hung from the ceiling in Allen's "Upside Down Room." (In the photo at right, Allen gives him last minute instructions.) That gag provided a great visual, but few laughs. It turned out that folks entering the room—where everything that should have been on the floor was hanging from the ceiling—were so stunned that they became temporarily speechless.

One of Allen's favorite elements in Candid Camera as the show evolved in the sixties were the discussions with children. "When I first considered including kids on our show," he recalled, "there was great resistance." Sponsors and network executives wondered how many youngsters would be watching a show that came on at 10 p.m. Allen argued that these sequences were *about* kids, not *for* kids. "Eventually they allowed us to try a piece and the response was overwhelming. From then on, children became a rich source of material and one of the most popular features of the show."

There are many favorites among the Candid Kids, but one standout was Allen's conversation with a girl who joined him in acting out "Cinderella"—she as Cinderella and he the prince.

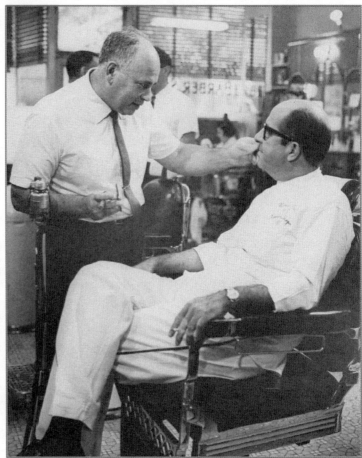

From top left: Allen and "Cinderella"; Phil Silvers plays an annoying barber; the lovable Lassie visits the studio; in New Orleans, glamorous Jayne Mansfield chats with Allen before her guest appearance.

Allen with Yogi Berra and Mickey Mantle; below on set with Buster Keaton.

Today, the phrase, "Smile, you're on Candid Camera," is widely known as one of the most popular slogans in TV history. But Allen never uttered the words until his show was in its 16th year. As much as audiences loved the show, there continued to be some critics who insisted that it was mean-spirited and too harsh (quite a laughable conclusion based on today's so-called "reality TV").

Allen was looking for a way to counter that; to underscore the idea that Candid Camera was good-natured fun. And so came the famous line, used to close each program and as part of a new theme song:

When it's least expected,
You're elected!
You're the star today...
Smile! You're on Candid Camera.
With our hocus-pocus,
You're in focus!
It's your lucky day...
Smile! You're on Candid Camera.

Peter as the statue in a New York art gallery.

And the memorable lyric went on to stress that laughing at yourself is "a tonic, tried and true." The new song helped propel Candid Camera to its highest ratings ever in 1962-63.

Despite holding so many records for longevity and creativity in television, Candid Camera has never won an Emmy award. Nor, for that matter has the show won any of the more prestigious showbiz awards such as a Golden Globe or Peabody. Allen always said it was because Candid Camera was so far ahead of its time that it fit no particular TV category.

But Allen did once receive an honor from a major plumbing supply group. It somehow determined that the phrase, "Smile, you're on Candid Camera," was the most popular graffiti in public restrooms.

In 1966, after five seasons as Allen's sidekick, Durward Kirby went off to perform in a Broadway play. What Allen missed most in losing Durward was that, "it seemed his taste was about the same as that of America's television audience. I felt that if Durward understood a gag and enjoyed it, America would get it."

For what turned out to be the final season of the CBS run in the sixties, Allen turned to Bess Myerson—former Miss America and talented pianist and author. She was the first of what network officials liked to call "promotable females," sharing the hosting with Allen and then in later years with Peter.

"The fact that Bess was Jewish, beautiful and brilliant made it a challenge to get her on the show," said Allen. "It's always been my opinion that brilliant women have an especially difficult time in life. This is because society, particularly back then, encouraged them to hide their true abilities so men didn't feel threatened. This was Bess's problem."

Times and attitudes have certainly changed over the decades. Peter's recent co-host, Mayim Bialik, is a PhD and a talented woman who qualifies as Jewish, beautiful and brilliant.

During the CBS run in the sixties Allen hired a secretary named Marilyn, who emerged as a successful performer in several Candid Camera gags and also became Allen's second wife. Allen and Marilyn had two children, Juliet and William— each of whom has also appeared on the show— before divorcing in 1978.

Bess Myerson, former Miss America, joined Allen for one season.

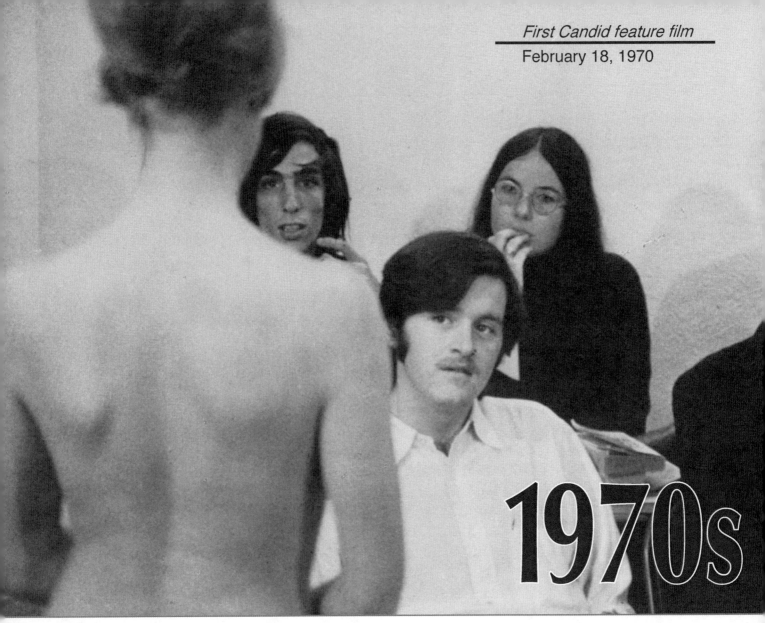

1970s

Allen liked to point out that "What Do You Say to a Naked Lady?" was, "the cleanest dirty movie ever made."

Following his CBS series, which completed its run in 1967, Allen was determined to break new ground with material that couldn't be shown on broadcast television. "Naked Lady" provided the chance to study our inhibitions about sex in an entertaining and yet mature way. It had nudity—resulting in an "X" rating—but the film was quite tame, even by the standards back then.

Critics were confused and the reviews went off in many directions. *The Bergen Record* in New Jersey said it was "perhaps the funniest movie of the year" (although, in fairness, it opened in mid-February). *Newsday's* critic said it was "pretty funny and even a little intelligent." The *N.Y. Post* concluded, "Whether you take it as simply sex stimulant or insight as to degrees of sexual freedom, generation gap, self-control, sex drive, it is unique and fascinating."

The Chicago Tribune praised "Naked Lady" as "a fresh look at stale attitudes." On the other hand, *The Chicago Daily News* called the film crude and clumsy and asked, "What's Funt trying to prove with this stupid set-up?"

The San Francisco Chronicle noted, "It is almost certain to be the most misunderstood, misjudged" film of the year. And so it went.

"What Do You Say to a Naked Lady?" did surprisingly well at the box office, despite the X rating. In assessing his film, Allen reported, "We found that while the Sexual Revolution had changed many young people, older people still

Above, college students react to a nude lecturer in "What Do You Say to a Naked Lady?"; at right, an actor eats cash in a scene from "Money Talks."

seemed to be living with almost-Victorian moral standards."

Despite its success, United Artists was slow to order the next Candid Camera film. Only after Allen agreed to co-fund the project was the green light received for "Money Talks." Released in 1972, the movie humorously looked at our views about the Almighty Buck—from a furrier asked to make an expensive coat for a Great Dane, to a guy at a lunch counter casually eating dollar bills.

The movie received some good reviews, including a near-rave in the showbiz paper *Variety*, but some felt that unlike "Naked Lady" it was too much like the Candid Camera TV series to stand alone as a full-length theatrical film. "Money Talks" flopped at the box office and was yanked from theaters before even earning back its costs of production. As if that wasn't bad enough, Allen discovered that his trusted accountant had been

CANDID TRIVIA: Costing only $570,000 to make, "Naked Lady" grossed well over $5 million in theaters.

stealing from him over a four-year period and had made off with roughly $3 million! The man eventually pleaded guilty and, the night before sentencing, checked into a New York City hotel and killed himself.

It was a difficult period for Allen: his second movie had done poorly, his accountant stole all of his money, and his marriage with Marilyn was on the rocks. Marital problems at least provided the inspiration for a third Candid Camera movie, this time made-for-TV. "Smile When You Say I Do" was broadcast on ABC-TV in 1973 and was a successful look at love and marriage, and it paved the way for Allen's return to television.

In television, one good thing usually leads to another, and so the Candid Camera film about marriage quickly resulted in an ABC special celebrating Candid Camera's 25th anniversary, which, in turn, opened the door to a new series for syndication, totaling 130 episodes between 1974 and 1979.

For its first season the series was taped in New York City, with John Bartholomew Tucker, a veteran of TV commercials and local news, as Allen's co-host. The following year, to cut costs, the "New" Candid Camera was taped before an audience at Opryland in Nashville. The co-host for the second season was former Miss America Phyllis George (pictured below with Allen), who was known for her work as a sports reporter on CBS-TV.

Except for occasional fill-in hosts, the balance of the series was co-hosted by Jo Ann Pflug, an actress with credits in numerous sitcoms and TV dramas. Returning as a regular in the field was comedienne and author Fannie Flagg, who first worked on Candid Camera in 1965 and was a viewer favorite for two decades.

The 70s series also marked the start of Candid Camera hosts with well-known spouses. Phyllis George was married to the Hollywood producer Robert Evans, and then to Kentucky Governor John Y. Brown, Jr. Jo Ann Pflug was the wife of TV game show host Chuck Woolery.

Years later, Peter Funt was partnered with Suzanne Somers, whose husband Alan Hamel was a noted talk show host in Canada. She was followed on the show by Dina Eastwood, wife of perhaps the most famous of the bunch: actor and director Clint Eastwood.

Although the weekly series was taped in Nashville, Candid Camera's production office remained in New York—necessitating lots of last-minute flights by producer Dick Briglia and others on the staff. Further complicating matters was that Allen had undertaken a search of the western states, seeking to buy a ranch.

By the time the final episode ran in 1979, Allen had moved his operation to California, with offices in Monterey and Hollywood.

Candid Confederates

A national magazine once named Allen Funt one of "The 10 Most Recognizable People in America." Yet, he earned his living playing everyday parts in everyday places—in real life. Pictured above are four of Candid Camera's undercover gag men, and all four are Allen Funt himself.

1980s

For Candid Camera the 1980s were something special, which is to say the decade was highlighted by a plethora of network TV specials. Remarkably, two of the specials were anniversary celebrations—the 35th, broadcast by NBC in 1983 (with Allen and Loni Anderson, pictured below) and the 40th, carried by CBS in 1987.

It was also the decade in which Peter joined Allen in shooting the Candid Camera scenes as well as co-hosting the specials. "Dad was based in Hollywood and I was in Connecticut," Peter recalls. "So we divided up the country. He took everything west of the Hollywood Freeway and gave me the rest."

The decade provided an eclectic mix in terms of Candid Camera's content. In addition to the two anniversary retrospectives, Allen produced an NBC special titled "The Difference Between Men and Women" in 1983, with co-hosts Loni Anderson and Valerie Harper. In 1985 he did a special for NBC titled "Candid Kids," with Nancy NcKeon. After the 40th anniversary show things really got going with a Christmas special (1987), a special about food (1988) and specials about cars and money (both in 1989).

While all this was happening on broadcast TV, Allen was also producing an adult version known as "Candid, Candid Camera," for HBO and then Playboy, as well as a version for home video—seeking to capture some of the magic that came from the movie "What Do You Say to a Naked Lady?"

CANDID TRIVIA: *Few TV series are able to mount an anniversary special, but Candid Camera has already had five— the 25th, 35th, 40th and 50th—so far.*

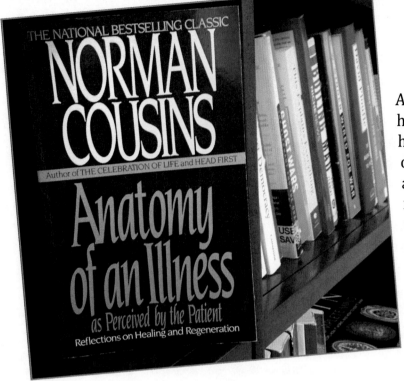

His experience with Laughter Therapy led Allen to think further about the impact of humor in our lives. "When a tragedy occurs," he noted, "people often feel the presence of humor is suddenly inappropriate. Their attitude seems to say, 'This is no laughing matter.' But I feel the opposite. I believe that laughing matters, and it's more essential for me in the tough times than ever."

As the 1980s moved on, Candid Camera's specials moved from NBC to CBS. (Remarkably, Candid Camera has appeared over the decades in prime-time on three of the major broadcast networks—ABC, NBC and CBS.)

The 40th anniversary special included a piece on Laughter Therapy, with appearances by both Norman Cousins and Paul Newman.

During this stretch, Allen gave up the use of a studio audience—in fact, he gave up the entire studio. As Peter explains: "We were each working out of our homes at the time, me in Rowayton, Connecticut, and Dad in Hollywood. My garage was filled with Candid Camera props and his basement was made into an editing room.

"When it came time to do the host portions I flew to Hollywood and we shot them in and around his house. Fortunately, Dad had a very photogenic house and garden that provided attractive backgrounds." *[On the opposite page, Allen directs a scene in the atrium at his home in Hollywood.]*

Another twist in the 80s was that Allen and Peter began wearing tuxedos on every show. "It made for some unusual juxtapositions," says Peter. "I might be standing in the driveway introducing a sequence about cars, and yet I'm in a tux. I did one with the actress Morgan Brittany in which we were in the back room at a paint store. The strangest, I think, was the time "Downtown" Julie Brown and I were on the 18th green at a golf course—and we're both dressed in formal attire, like we're headed to the prom!"

The formal attire remained as a trademark

One of Allen's proudest accomplishments in the 1980s was the formation of his non-profit known as Laughter Therapy. The idea was born after noted author Norman Cousins chronicled the physical benefits he obtained while seriously ill by watching Candid Camera films. "I made the joyous discovery," Cousins wrote, "that ten minutes of genuine belly laughter had an anesthetic effect that would give me at least two hours of pain-free sleep."

Among those moved by what Cousins wrote was film star Paul Newman, who contacted Allen on behalf of the director John Huston, suffering with a painful form of cancer. Huston reported that 30 minutes of Candid Camera viewing gave him as much as four hours without pain.

These reports, along with statements by far lesser-known people, inspired Allen to launch his foundation, sending specially selected Candid Camera tapes to critically ill people at no charge. Peter and the Candid Camera staff continue the Laughter Therapy operation to this day.

CANDID TRIVIA: The money to launch Laughter Therapy came from a former staffer who wrote a book in which she told lies about Allen. As restitution, she paid to start the foundation.

for the Funts throughout the 1980s and into the early 90s.

In addition to cable shows and network specials, Allen found time in the early 80s to teach a psychology course at Monterey Peninsula College near his home in Central California. Using clips from the show, he illustrated behavioral concepts including group pressure, vanity and honesty. He also covered what's known as "cognitive dissonance," which occurs when someone is confronted by contradictory or unbelievable circumstances.

"For example," Allen told his students, "a man comes into a corridor and finds there are two doors that he can use. One is marked, 'Use Other Door,' and the other one says, 'Danger Do Not Enter.'" For some, the anxiety caused by such an impossible choice is almost unbearable.

Allen also cited two "major themes" that he had observed over years of shooting Candid Camera. The first is *Herd-Mindedness*: "People are easily led anywhere by a strong hand," he notes. "Once I walked up a down escalator and soon everyone was following. They said I seemed to know where I was going."

Next is *Obedience to Authority*: "We once closed the state of Delaware, and people accepted it. We placed a sign on a floor with black and white squares instructing people to step only on the black squares, and they did!"

In an interview with *The New York Times*, Allen said he took the teaching gig, "to do something I've always believed in, which is to use humor for education. When people are smiling, they're receptive to almost anything you want to teach them."

1990s

As the decade began, Allen produced more specials on CBS, plus a summer series of half-hour episodes. These were themed Candid Camera shows, which Peter hosted along with weekly guest co-hosts such as comedienne Victoria Jackson and actresses Audrey Landers, Morgan Brittany and Julie McCullough. *[Pictured above are Peter, Allen and Julie, taping in Nassau for the "On Vacation" show.]*

"It was hectic but fun shooting this batch of shows," Peter recalls. "We were traveling to many locations and testing different themes—which was great. However, I was given a different lady to work with in each show, so I never really got to know them or develop any special chemistry.

"Audrey Landers, who played Afton Cooper on 'Dallas,' was the hardest to get to know because her mother always stood a few feet away on the set. Victoria Jackson, known best for her work on

'Saturday Night Live,' actually taught me lot. Once I was so distracted trying to produce a Candid Camera scene with her at a hospital in Connecticut that I really didn't pay attention when one of the people we photographed wanted to talk briefly. Victoria really let me have it. She said the least I could do was give the guy a minute or two—and it was something I never forgot.

"Victoria also taught me about loosening up on TV. We were doing the 'goodbyes,' you know: 'Don't be surprised...' All of a sudden she starts dancing and singing our theme song. After the take I said, 'We can't do that. We've got to be straight.' Of course, my father wound up using her version on the air and it was perfect."

In 1990 the trade publication *Variety* wrote, "The latest new Candid Camera specials seem to be getting funnier." A year later, they added that the CBS shows were "bringing back the energy of

CANDID TRIVIA: Candid Camera has always been "low budget," in TV terms, but in 1990 the cost of a single show topped $500,000 for the first time.

the show's earlier years."

Allen was busier than ever in the early 90s, tending to his 1,100-acre cattle ranch at Big Sur in California, in addition to producing the shows in Hollywood. He also began working on his life story in the book "Candidly, Allen Funt," which was published by Barricade Books in 1994.

"I've always thought that while Candid Camera is successful, it is misunderstood," Allen wrote. "The fact that so many others have tried to copy our format and failed is proof of this."

There were two poor "copies" of Candid Camera in the early 90s—and one was authorized by the Funts themselves. The first, completely unauthorized, was a Fox series titled "Hidden Video." Before the first show aired, Peter got hold of the pilot and couldn't believe what he saw: friends of his from college who were now professional comedians had been hired by the Fox show to *pretend* they were caught by hidden cameras. The show was a fake. Allen sued but was unable to stop the project, although Fox did promise to use only "real" people and to change the title to "Totally Hidden Video" (as if that mattered).

The second rip-off was actually a co-venture between Allen and the King World company. It resulted in a daily syndicated version of Candid Camera, hosted by Dom DeLuise. Allen, who was misled about his creative role, called it "a complete embarrassment," adding, "I was relieved when the show went off the air in a relatively short time."

Peter poses as an umpire in a real minor-league game. The pitcher was stymied because his catcher was purposely giving fake signs.

In 1993, Allen suffered a serious stroke while working at his office in Hollywood. That led to many months of hospitalization and then rehab in Los Angeles. When he was finally able to go home, Allen retired to his house in Pebble Beach, California, and to his ranch some 20 miles south at Big Sur. It marked the end of the CBS network specials, at least temporarily.

Allen's ranch, with the landmark Bixby Bridge connecting the property on both sides of the famed Highway One, was a jewel. In his memoir, Allen described the first time he saw the ranch property: "I looked over the edge of a cliff and down to the ocean. Two enormous rocks jutted out of the water, and the waves foamed around them. [Moving inland] The road gently descended between two broad mountains toward a weathered barn and several outbuildings. Then the road climbed again through pastures and groves of pine and cypress until it disappeared out of sight in the distance. Cattle grazed here and there and a colt frisked in a wooded corral."

Allen was not the retiring kind, but when it did come time to slow down, the ranch was a marvelous setting and brought him great joy.

It was shortly thereafter that Peter [*pictured below with Allen at the ranch*] took over as president of the Candid Camera company. There were many loose ends, including the failed version by King World as well as a theft by a Hollywood broker, who illegally sold Candid Camera reruns to outlets around the globe.

The legal entanglements, along with the task of caring for Allen's health, his business interests and his properties, took up a lot of time over a stretch of three years.

Allen's retirement created a hectic and strange scene at his Pebble Beach house, which doubled as a production office for Peter and the new members of Candid Camera's staff. "It was kind of like a sitcom," says Peter. "One minute one of us would be editing a piece of tape and the next we'd be pushing Dad around the neighborhood in a wheelchair. The staff included an editor, a producer and a production secretary, plus a nurse, a cook and a physical therapist—and we each learned how to do most of the different jobs.

"Adding to the bizarre nature of things was the fact that community rules prohibited us from operating a business from the house. We'd get periodic complaints about the number of cars, and odd looks from neighbors who wondered how it could be that a single retiree needed so many companions."

The crowd grew larger every time Allen's kids and grandchildren came to visit. His daughter Patricia and son John live in Connecticut, while daughter Juliet and son William live in Los Angeles. Peter and his wife Amy, along with their kids, Stephanie and Danny, moved to California to try to coordinate the business and family affairs.

By 1995, Peter was developing some new ideas for Candid Camera along with a plan to mark the show's 50th anniversary with a new network special.

Celebrating Allen's 78th birthday in 1992, at a hotel in Italy, are: (standing from left) William, Patricia, her daughter Katie and husband Ken; John, Juliet, Peter and wife Amy; (seated) Anne Flynn, Allen and Peter's daughter Stephanie.

Candid Camera's 50th Anniversary
CBS: August 29, 1996

When Candid Camera needed a jump start in the mid-90s it was again an anniversary special that did the trick. It had happened before—with the 25th and 40th anniversary shows—and now it was the 50th birthday celebration that paved the way for a new collection of network specials and then an entirely new weekly series.

The program ran on a Thursday night in late August, CBS's toughest slot of the week. Peter was teamed with Leeza Gibbons, who at the time was hosting her own talk show. The response was remarkable, with the trade paper *Variety* calling it "the upset of the night." *The Hollywood Reporter* added, "It was the first time that CBS had won that hour since August 4, 1994."

And the reviews were terrific. People said it was "a hilarious half-century's worth of pranks." *The New York Times* critic said, "I defy you to keep a straight face." *TV Guide* asked, "Can it be we've underestimated Candid Camera?"

A short time later, the show was back in full production as CBS ordered four new specials for 1997. Unfortunately, Leeza's bosses at Paramount refused to allow her to continue co-hosting the show, so CBS picked a lesser-known TV host named Lorianne Crook, who at the time was just launching a new syndicated talk show.

The shows with Lorianne were well received but when it came time to do a special called "The Battle of Sexes" CBS decided to switch to someone with an abundance of, well, sex appeal. The network had Suzanne Somers under contract and she seemed like the perfect fit.

"I met Suzanne for the first time on a location in Beverly Hills," recalls Peter. "I was beginning to think that everyone I'd ever work with would be represented by their husband. We had talked to Mary Hart of 'ET' and her husband, Burt Sugarman handled the negotiations. Then we found that Lorianne was repped by her husband, the Nashville producer Jim Owens. And Suzanne is, of course, managed by her husband Alan Hamel.

"Fortunately, Alan is a straight shooter. He drives a hard bargain, but he's fair. So, it didn't take long to complete the deal for Suzanne—

making her the longest-running female co-host in Candid Camera's history."

"The Battle of the Sexes" was a huge hit on CBS when it ran in the fall of 1997. What came next was a dream come true:

"The night 'Battle' was telecast," says Peter, "Amy and I were on vacation in Virginia. At lunch the next day I excused myself to call the CBS phone in Hollywood that carried the recorded Nielsen ratings information. I couldn't believe my ears as the numbers were rattled off by a pre-Siri voice. The ratings were better than I had hoped.

"Six hours later I had to excuse myself from dinner—this time to take a call. The CBS vice president on the line said the network wanted to make Candid Camera a weekly series. And, just like that, we took our place, Friday at 8:30 p.m., returning to the CBS schedule for the first time since Dad signed off in 1967."

CBS series premiere
February 27, 1998

How did the new series differ from Allen's classic approach? Peter and the team were determined to stay faithful to the formula, but the sequences were now slightly shorter and there were one or two more of them in a half-hour show. The new edition also tried to show more people in each situation and more "reveals"—those magical moments when people are told, "Smile! You're on Candid Camera."

Like the 60s version, the new show developed a team of engaging players in the field. Kate McNamara and Linda Tosetti were favorites, along with New York producer Dick Briglia, who had worked with Allen in the 70s and now was back performing in sequences.

"I was very proud of this team," says Peter. "That includes our key camera people as well: Todd Simon, Ira Speir and Chris Angelos. Our show isn't easy. I recall once shooting in a hotel room where people arrived to find a donkey tied to the bed. Ira was hiding with his camera in a small closet, but he was allergic to the donkey and the straw we put on the ground. Imagine shooting for eight or ten hours and worrying the whole time that you're about to sneeze!"

Peter and his co-hosts in the 90s. On opposite page, Leeza Gibbons. This page, top, Lorianne Crook; bottom, Suzanne Somers.

Opposite: Peter tricks the Oakland Raiders cheerleaders with new, ugly uniforms; a courtroom scene in Denver. This page, clockwise from top left, Susan Anton "buys" a town; Little Richard records the Candid Camera theme; a chimp poses as a human baby, and Ray Romano offers smiles.

A few days short of his 85th birthday, Allen passed away in 1999 from complications related to the stroke he had suffered six years earlier. He died peacefully at his home in Pebble Beach with Peter at his side.

"I held his hand and promised to take care of the family and the show," said Peter. "He had impressed us all in those final years with his spirit, and when it was time to go he just slipped away."

The next morning's Monterey Herald had as its lead headline: MAN WITH A SMILE DIES.

Allen's ashes were scattered at his ranch. He wasn't a religious man and he left no instructions about how his passing would be handled. The family decided to hold a memorial at a spot in Hollywood that was symbolic in a funny kind of way: Mel's Diner on Sunset Boulevard.

"It was a perfect setting," Peter explains. "Dad always loved shooting sequences in diners; he must have done dozens over the years. We also spent hours at Mel's working on ideas for the show. Once Dad was enjoying a bowl of matzo ball soup when he said out of the blue, 'What would happen in a baseball game if the catcher gave the pitcher signals that he had never seen before? Would the guy ever throw a pitch?'

"That's just the way my father's mind worked, and after we kicked it around I went to Jamestown, N.Y., where a minor-league team let us do that exact gag, with great results."

The memorial luncheon at Mel's included loving statements from Allen's five kids: Patricia, John, Juliet, William and Peter. Guests included Suzanne Somers and her husband Alan, and even the mayor of Carmel, Ken White.

Many tributes came in—from famous people Allen had worked with, but also from hundreds of ordinary folks he had photographed over the years, or just gifted with a smile as they sat in front of the TV. And there was a long list of newspaper obituaries, among them:

New York Times: *Allen Funt has been described as part humorist, psychologist and con artist who honed his act to a fine art over four decades.*

The San Francisco Chronicle: *Allen Funt's gift was to realize that human nature didn't need a rewrite. People were funny in their most natural roles—as themselves.*

Chicago Tribune: *Funt's gags were always in good fun. His situations were embarrassing and mischievous, but never vicious.*

A tribute to Allen was entered into the Congressional Record by Rep. Sam Farr of California. It read in part:

Mr. Speaker, I rise today to honor a man who with boundless energy and enthusiasm spread laughter throughout the nation with his long-running TV show Candid Camera.

He was a visionary who pioneered what has become an entire programming genre, but who also genuinely cared about people and appreciated the healing power of laughter. Allen donated his entire film library to the psychology department of his alma mater, Cornell University, in order to share his insights into the human psyche. After settling in the Monterey Peninsula in 1978, Allen held fundraisers to support Carmel schools in the 1980s and donated tapes to hospitals and the homes of the terminally ill.

Allen Funt was truly a remarkable man who will be fondly remembered for his ingenuity and enthusiasm. Allen will be missed by the countless numbers of people he touched both personally and through his Candid Camera show around the world.

2000s

As the new century began, Candid Camera was continuing its successful run on the CBS weekly schedule. The shows were taped before an audience in Hollywood, where the show maintained a production office, but half the staff worked out of a field office in Pacific Grove in Central California, about 325 miles away.

"It was a bit hectic, flying down to LA to tape each show and then rushing back to prepare the next one," Peter recalls. "But it was nice because it allowed me to be home as much as possible with Amy and our kids, Stephanie and Danny."

Peter believed it was critical for Candid Camera to travel to as many parts of the country as possible each week. "The whole premise of our show is that you never know where we'll turn up next—so to re-enforce that we went to all 50

CANDID TRIVIA: *Before joining Peter on Candid Camera, Dina went by her maiden name, Ruiz, as a news anchor on KSBW-TV in Salinas, California.*

states and tried to include as many different locations as we could."

The show relied on New York-based producer Dick Briglia to cover as much of the Northeast as he could, while Peter's crews branched out to the rest of the country from California. Suzanne, although at first reluctant to do sequences out in the field, became accomplished at ad-libbing for a variety of hidden-camera scenes. One of the funniest was when she played the part of a bride-to-be who swallows her engagement ring.

After three-plus seasons on the weekly schedule, CBS decided to return Candid Camera to a format of periodic specials. Peter had a tough choice to make: accept CBS's offer, or continue doing the weekly series on the cable channel known as PAX.

The decision was to continue as a weekly series with the same format, studio and creative team. Unfortunately, with a smaller budget Peter was no longer able to keep Suzanne as co-host.

"That was rough," Peter explains. "I loved working with Suzanne and viewers were rooting for her as well. I thought if we had to go in a different direction we might as well try someone who wasn't as well known but who could really grow into the Candid Camera role."

Luck was on Peter's side since his new partner was living just a few miles away in Pebble Beach: Dina Eastwood, who was married at the time to the famous actor and director Clint Eastwood.

"Dina had done some local TV and I had gotten to know her a bit in connection with local charities," says Peter. "We brought her to our studio in Hollywood to do one show as sort of a test, and she was great. We stayed together for several years, through the PAX run.

"Of course, I'd be lying if I said her married name didn't help with publicity. And it didn't hurt one bit that Clint was able to get us travel on the Warner Bros. jet, as well as a chance to play in some major golf tournaments—including a few times as Clint's partner. That was intimidating. I learned that Clint's main goal in golf is playing quick-

ly. He likes to win, of course, but he really values speed, and if you're his partner, you'd better not linger too long over your shots!"

Unlike Suzanne's husband Alan, who attended every taping, Clint only visited Candid Camera's studio a few times, keeping a low profile. "I mostly got to see him on the flights back to Monterey," says Peter. "Once, I couldn't believe my eyes as Clint boarded the plane carrying a baby pig. It seems the Eastwoods had several farm animals as pets at their home, and this was the latest addition. That day it was in Clint's arms, but I'm told the pig eventually grew to weigh several hundred pounds.

"I tried for weeks but I couldn't come up with a proper gag that would feature a pig."

Allen's grandchildren got into the act in the 2000s, as owners of a lemonade stand with undrinkably bad lemonade. From left, Anna, Stephanie, Danny and Katie.

A major project in the 2000s was producing a 10-DVD collection of Candid Camera's best shows and clips. The package was released on the Rhino label at Warner Bros.

For the set, Peter produced a video called "Greatest Moments," featuring the best sequences from Candid Camera's library, most in their original length. Also included is Allen's complete 1949 show in which the name Candid Camera was used for the first time.

The set features dozens of complete episodes, which were assembled and curated by Bill Funt.

Other DVDs were also produced, beyond the Rhino collection, including Peter and Dina's "Most Requested Characters" and "The Funt Family Collection," featuring the show's "Biggest Surprises" and smiles with "Pets & Animals."

During the decade many imitations of Candid Camera came and went on TV. "I suppose if imitation is the sincerest form of flattery," notes Peter, "then you'd have to say that my family and I are extremely flattered.

"But the fact is much of what is now called 'Reality TV' is not at all what my Dad would have favored. Some is quite mean-spirited. On our show we have always been careful not to push too hard or go too far.

"The worst hidden-camera copies seem designed to prove that people are fools. I don't think that's true; people are by and large good sports and willing to take a joke at their own expense."

In 2008 Peter added a new outlet for his observations about the world and human nature: a syndicated newspaper column. The columns, which can also be found at CandidCamera.com, cover a wide range of topics. Some have run in *The New York Times* and *Wall Street Journal*, and are collected in the book, "Cautiously Optimistic."

In a box designed like a television camera, the 10-disc set was the centerpiece of the home video collection, released by Rhino in 2005.

A Scrapbook of Smiles

2010s

Candid Camera resumed production in mid-decade with a series of 10 hourlong shows for TV Land. This time Peter was teamed with sitcom star Mayim Bialik, known to viewers for her role as Amy on the hit CBS series "The Big Bang Theory."

Much of the production team was happily reunited—from producer Kate McNamara, to tape editors Bill Cartwright, Bob Franco and Ray Miller, to field producer Linda Tosetti, to directors Ron de Moraes and Lenn Goodside, plus many other familiar faces. The shows were taped on the same lot in Hollywood where the Candid Camera specials were shot in the 1990s.

"It was really pleasing to be back," says Peter. "Candid Camera's remarkable longevity has set many records in television, yet who would have thought the same team could pull this off again?"

Viewers immediately welcomed the chemistry between Peter and Mayim. Her banter before and after sequences was pleasingly spontaneous and clever.

Mayim played the young Bette Midler in the film "Beaches" at age 12 and was just 16 when she starred in the NBC sitcom "Blossom," so like Peter she grew up in showbiz. She's clearly the most well-educated host Candid Camera has ever had. She earned a BS from UCLA in 2000 in Neuroscience and Hebrew & Jewish Studies, and went on to the Ph.D. program in Neuroscience, also at UCLA. Mayim has written two books and is a frequent speaker on college campuses.

The stage set for the TV Land series was designed by Jimmy Cuomo, who designed the set for the earlier series on CBS and PAX. This time the idea was to use a news-style desk with large monitors. Jimmy's first sketch, above, was completed before Mayim was hired, so Jimmy placed two males at the desk.

For the TV Land episodes, a third generation of Funts got to participate. Peter's son Danny and Patricia's daughter Katie Oxman each did some funny sequences—for instance, Danny getting New Yorkers to sign a fake political petition and Katie playing the part of a supermarket cashier who wouldn't stop talking on her cell phone.

"I was born after Grandpa's great career," says Danny, "but I've viewed many hours of his work on DVDs. And I grew up watching my father do the show, so to be able to actually try my hand at this unique type of TV is an epic experience."

The TV Land episodes got good reviews and scored well in the ratings. Yet, when it came time to produce more shows, TV Land underwent a change in programming and replaced many of its key executives, leaving Candid Camera on the sidelines.

"It's too bad," explains Peter, "because we were somewhat rushed to complete the ten shows and everyone thought we were really in a good spot to go forward. But television is a tricky business and so many of the puzzle pieces have to fit. I'm just glad we got to do what we did, and I'm looking forward to our next opportunity with a different network."

Meanwhile, Peter and his producer, Brian Courrejou, embarked on yet another form of Candid Camera fun, by literally taking the show on the road. Beginning in 2015 they traveled to theaters around the country with a stage show called, "8 Decades of Smiles." The unique production combines Peter's comedy and anecdotes with the funniest clips from the vast Candid Camera library. The result is two-plus hours of fun for audiences of all ages.

So, what's next for Candid Camera? Will it be a 70th anniversary special? Some new twist on the famous format?

"Everywhere we travel now with the stage show," says Peter, "people ask when we'll be back on the air with new shows. It's amazing, really, that Dad's single idea—catching people 'in the act of being themselves,' as he used to put it, has endured for so long.

"And there were some other lines he enjoyed using, such as, 'You go your way, and we'll go your way too.' Which I guess brings us to: 'Don't be surprised if sometime, somewhere, some place when you least expect it, someone steps up to you and says: Smile! You're on Candid Camera!'"

CANDID TRIVIA: At the stage show in Fort Collins, Colo., Peter got a severe nose bleed and did the entire show holding a tissue to his face. Half the audience was certain it was a Candid Camera gag!

Made in the USA
Columbia, SC
17 March 2023

13946906R00027